D1325384

Passions

Glimpses
of
Romance

by
Patrick Caton

Cover Photo © John Running/
Tony Stone Images
Cover Design and Typography by Roy Honegger

Published by Great Quotations Publishing Co.,
Glendale Heights, IL

Library of Congress Catalog Card
Number: 96-76126

ISBN 1-56245-273-8

Printed in Hong Kong

*T*love thee with breath,
Smiles, tears, of all my life.

—Elizabeth Barrett Browning

*N*ever underestimate the
power of passion.

—*Eve Sawyer*

$\mathcal{G}$row old along with me!
The best is yet to be,
The last of life for which
the first was made.

—*Robert Browning*

*I*f you'd be loved,
be worthy to be loved.

—*Ovid*

$\mathscr{T}$hrice happy they whom
an unbroken bond unites,
And whom no quarrel shall
sunder before life's final day.

—Horace

*I*f you would be loved, love.

—*Hecato*

*H*ow do I love thee?
Let me count the ways.
I love thee to the depth
and breadth and height
My soul can reach.

—*Elizabeth Barrett Browning*

*B*ut happy they!
The happiest of their kind!
Whom gentler stars unite,
and in one fate
Their hearts, their fortunes,
and their beings blend.

—*Samuel Taylor Coleridge*

*A*s your wedding ring wears,
You'll wear off your cares.

—*Thomas Fuller*

*F*or I do love you…
as the dew loves the flowers;
as the birds love the sunshine;
as the wavelets love the breeze.

—*Mark Twain*

$\mathcal{G}$od the best maker
of all marriages
Combine your hearts in one.

—*Shakespeare*

$\mathscr{L}$ove is always in the mood
of believing in miracles.

—*John Cowper Powys*

$\mathcal{W}$hat's the earth
With all its art, verse, music, worth-
Compared with love found,
gained, and kept?

—*Robert Browning*

*O*ne year of joy, another of comfort,
and all the rest of content.

—*John Ray*

$\mathcal{T}$he most precious possession that ever comes to a man in this world is a woman's heart.

—*Holland*

$\mathcal{I}$ like not only to be loved,
but to be told I am loved.

—George Eliot

*W*e always believe our first love is our last, and our last love our first.

—*George Whyte-Melville*

*T*wo souls with but a single
thought, two hearts
that beat as one.

—*von Munch Bellinghausen*

$\mathcal{O}$f all the music that reached
farthest into heaven, it is the
beating of a loving heart.

—*Henry Ward Beecher*

$\mathcal{T}$here are so many ways to love,
and each one has its own delights.

—*Sara Teasdale*

*L*ove does not consist of gazing at each other but in looking outward together in the same direction.

—*Antoine de Saint-Exupéry*

*I*t is not sex that gives the
pleasure, but the lover.

—*Marge Piercy*

*T*here is nothing half so sweet
in life as love's young dreams.

—*Thomas Moore*

$\mathscr{D}$o you love me because I'm beautiful, or am I beautiful because you love me?

—*Oscar Hammerstein*

$\mathscr{I}$ hate being without you because
it's so easy to be with you.

—*Gail Lapekas*

*L*ove is an irresistible desire
to be irresistibly desired.

—*Robert Frost*

*T*here are two sorts of romantics:
those who love, and those who
love the adventure of loving.

—*Lesley Blanch*

*I*n real love you want
the other person's good.
In romantic love you want
the other person.

—*Margaret Anderson*

$\mathscr{N}$o temptation can ever be
measured by the value of its object.

—*Colette*

A caress is better than a career.

—*Elisabeth Marbury*

....*N*o one knows how it is
that with one glance a boy can
break through into a girl's heart.

—*Nancy Thayer*

𝒯he act of longing for something
will always be more intense
than the requiting of it.

—*Gail Godwin*

*T*he only passion sin can commit
is to be joyless.

—*Dorothy Sayers*

*A*bsence does not make
the heart grow fonder, but it
sure heats up the blood.

—*Elizabeth Ashley*

*I*n many ways do the
full heart reveal
The presence of love
it would conceal.

—*Samuel Taylor Coleridge*

$\mathcal{W}$e are minor in everything
but our passions.

—*Elizabeth Bowen*

*ℋ*ow love the limb-loosener
sweeps me away....

—*Sappho*

$\mathcal{T}$here is one who kisses,
and the other who offers a cheek.

—*French Proverb*

*L*ove is a butterfly, which when
pursued is just beyond your grasp,
but if you will sit down quietly
it may alight upon you.

—*Nathaniel Hawthorne*

$\mathcal{S}$ome things in life are so special
they are indescribable—
that's how I feel about us.

—*Gayle Lapekas*

*I*f I know what love is,
it is because of you.

—*Hermann Hesse*

$\mathcal{L}$ove: to feel with one's whole self the existence of another being.

—*Simone Weil*

$\mathscr{C}$ome love with me and
be my love; and we will
all the pleasures prove.

—*Christopher Marlowe*

*T*he best way to hold a man
is in your arms.

—*Mae West*

*K*isses kept are wasted;
love is to be tasted.

—*Edmund Vance*

$\mathscr{T}$he sound of a kiss is not so loud
as that of a cannon, but its echo
lasts a great deal longer.

—*Oliver Wendell Holmes*

*O*h, what lies there are in kisses!

—*Heinrich Heine*

$\mathcal{M}$y love is like a red, red rose
That's newly sprung in June;
Oh, my love is like the melody
That's sweetly played in tune.

—*Robert Burns*

$\mathscr{S}$ometimes idiosyncrasies which used to be irritating become endearing, part of the complexity of a partner who has become woven deep into our own selves.

—*Madeleine L'Engle*

*T*o enjoy a lifetime of romance—
fall in love with yourself.

—*Proverb*

*N*one so true as you and I...
Love like ours can never die!

—*Rudyard Kipling*

*L*ove me in full being.

—*Elizabeth Barrett Browning*

In short, I will part with
anything for you but you.

—*Lady Mary Wortley*

$\mathcal{L}$ove at the lips was touch
as sweet as I could bear.

—*Robert Frost*

*W*hatever our souls are made of,
his and mine are the same.

—*Emily Brontë*

*I*f I had never met him I would
have dreamed him into being.

—*Anzia Yezierska*

$\mathscr{L}$ove is like the magic
touch of stars.

—*Walter Benton*

*I*s it fair that you occupy
so many of my thoughts—
and so much of my heart?

—*Gayle Lapekas*

*T*here's plenty of fire
in the coldest flint!

—*Rachel Field*

*L*ove—bittersweet, irrepressible—
loosens my limbs and I tremble.

—Sappho

*B*laze with the fire that
is never extinguished.

—*Luisa Sigea*

63

... *W*ant, the Mistress of Invention,
still tempts me on...

—*Susannah Centlivre*